"70 Is  '

(Except When You Wanna DO Stuff!!!)

Like...

Walking

Running

Sleeping

Reading without squinting

Hearing when people talk softly

Having Sex

And other stuff...

A compilation of humorous but true stories by

Carole Blake

Author of "Help! My Face Has Fallen and it Can't Get Up!"

DENVER, COLORADO

Outskirts Press, Inc.
http://www.outskirtspress.com

ISBN: 978-1-4787-2692-0

Outskirts Press and the "OP" logo are trademarks belonging to Outskirts Press, Inc.

PRINTED IN THE UNITED STATES OF AMERICA

Table of Contents

1

OK...So I'm 70!

Thanks, Larry, for making 70 so special!

ON TURNING 70 - (2013)

How did this happen to me? One minute I'm learning how to ride a two-wheeler...and the next minute I'm filling out Social Security forms. I remember my Sweet Sixteen party at a beach club in Long Island where I grew up. And next month I'm having my 70th birthday party at a local restaurant. (This time I don't have to *sneak* a sip of wine! Actually, I might just drink the whole bottle!)

As I look back on my life, there are certain milestones which stand out: moving to Long Island from Brooklyn in time for third grade; graduating from high school; going to college in Philadelphia; living and working in New York City at a film company; meeting my (first) husband and getting married; giving birth to my daughter and my son; writing my first song and receiving an award for it; being an executive producer of a Hollywood movie; getting divorced; meeting Larry who soon happily became my husband; dealing with the death of my parents; attending my children's weddings; welcoming my three adorable grandsons; writing articles that were actually published; mourning the death of one of my closest friends; volunteering for 12 years as a mentor to 7 little girls who needed some extra help; trying Botox which – instead of improving my looks – actually caused my eyelids to droop; and finally, accepting myself – lines and all – as a Senior Citizen. Now *that's* living!

So...why do I sometimes feel blue? Well, maybe it's because I realize that it just can't go on like this forever! And then I ask myself, "Why think that way? Why not enjoy every minute of every day?" And so then I don't feel so blue! I have a blast playing tennis with my friends, and lately I'm hitting the ball harder than I have in years! I still love writing songs...and I'm still good at it! I'm writing *this* piece...right? And it's not half bad! (No need for the reader to comment here!) Larry tells me every day how much he loves me. That's not half bad either! OK...so I have a few (several) lines in my face. Who cares? Larry tells me that I'm beautiful. (Maybe he needs new glasses!) I'm lucky that I can still fit into a dress I have from years ago...size 6. Last time I was examined by a doctor I got a pretty good report...so no complaining there. I have fantastic friends who are supportive and loving, one of whom I've known since I was 2½ , and being an 'only child', that really means a lot to me.

Will there be new things to try in the coming years? Will any of my (hundreds of) songs turn into hits? Will I travel to new and different places? Will I enjoy romantic dinners at nice restaurants with my handsome husband? Will my grandsons enjoy my company as they're growing up? Gosh...I hope so!

So now...after thinking about all of this, today I say, "Come on SEVENTY??? BRING IT ON!!! I'm ready for the next chapter!

2

Adventures with My Friends

My College friends, Sue, Myra, me, and Marilyn – 40 years later!

My Grade School and High School friends, Me, Gerry, Nancy, and Ginger – 50 years later!

(Miss you, Nancy…)

A TENNIS "LOVE" LETTER - (2009)

I absolutely LOVE playing tennis! My Mom was a club-tennis champion in Baltimore in the 1930s…and she actually played tennis on the last day of her life at age 83. I was glad that one of her last memories was of a fun tennis doubles game. I learned the game at age 10 at a summer camp, and I've been playing socially ever since then.

I grew up in Long Island, and I learned how to play tennis at summer camp when I was 10. I think I was pretty good, but except for those camp summers, I really didn't play very much. And then, in my early 30s, after getting married, having two babies, and moving to Westchester, I was invited into a women's doubles game at a local indoor court. It was so much fun! I discovered the pluses and minuses of my own game: I had great placement of the ball; I was extremely steady (annoyingly so); I had the ability to hit a "dink" shot (whereby the ball just makes it over the net by about an inch) which my opponents found impossible to get; and "power shots" were definitely NOT my thing.

When I moved to the south shore of Long Island, I joined the Atlantic Beach Tennis Club which was one block from the beach. It had 13 beautifully maintained tennis courts and the most competitive middle aged women I had ever met. I have to admit: I was one of them. After many years of playing tennis…of my kids growing up…of getting a divorce… I met a very nice man at this tennis club. His name was Larry, and he had been recently separated as well. He was in a steady game with Red Holzman, the legendary beloved coach of the New York Knicks, and two other men. Larry and I started dating, and one day he and I challenged Red and his partner, Arnold, to a tennis game. Red was quite the celebrity at the time and he always played on whichever court he chose. Usually it was court #4, the one right by the revolving door. Well, on this day, court #4 was occupied, so we all went to court #6. We began our match, and Larry and I *creamed* them! But Mr. Holzman had a very reasonable explanation: "It was only because we *weren't* on court #4!" Hey, who's gonna argue with Red Holzman? We've had many good laughs about that.

When Larry and I moved to the Hamlet, a lovely condominium community on Long Island's north shore, I wanted to join the tennis team. It was the "A" Team, and luckily, the captain had called a woman she had known from Atlantic Beach Tennis to check up on my skills. I got the OK - cheap with only a thousand-buck-bribe (Only kidding!) - and I was on the team! I have totally enjoyed being on the team. I love the competition…the camaraderie…and, of course, the lunches after the matches! But who knew it would sometimes be like high school all over again!

So now I'm in my 60s, and I might not be as agile as I once was, but I think the *execution* of my shots is still pretty darn good. (Sometimes I'd like to *execute* my partner, but that's another story.) And as far as my "high school" reference, I mean that there's definitely an "in" group. Sometimes I'm *in* it; sometimes I'm *not!* We have 9 women on our team, and 6 of us play in any given Thursday match. Most of the time we play against tennis clubs or country clubs where the women are at least half our age. And we do pretty well, if I say so myself. In one of my most recent matches my partner kept whispering to me, "Keep it away from the 18-year-old!" So we hit to the 20-year-old, and…we *won!*

I hope I can play tennis forever. It's great exercise; it's wonderful competition; and maybe, unlike high school, I can be in the "popular" group!

Game…Set…Match!

THE OLD COLLEGE DAYS - (2009)

Recently I was thinking how very different things are in 2009 from the way they were in my college days. Today, every kid has *at least* a computer, a cell phone, an IPod, a Blackberry…*whatever!* When I was a freshman at Temple University in Philadelphia in 1961 (yikes!), I remember my very first day. My parents took me to the dorm where I had been assigned a roommate, and that's when I met "Lana of the Smelly Feet". Don't get me wrong…she was perfectly pleasant; it's just her *feet* that weren't! The 'aroma' kind of took over the entire room, and I was constantly concerned that the problem would rest at *my* feet! (Pardon the pun!) Anyway, after the first semester, when you were allowed to switch roommates…I did.

My dorm was called Peabody Hall, and my new roommate was a very good friend, and we had lots of other friends who lived down the hall. There were no phones in the rooms; there were three phones at the end of each hall. If there was a call for you, a buzzer would ring in your room, and you would run to a hallway phone. No one had a TV in their room; there was a TV in the lounge. Computers were not invented yet; if you had research to do for class, you went to the library.

I really don't know much about college dating today, but back then it was very common for a freshman to be "fixed up" on a blind date by an upper classman. One day a senior girl approached me and told me that she was giving my name to some guy she knew. I was flattered and said, "Sure". The next day my buzzer rang. I ran to the (hall) phone, and I was talking to my 'blind-date-guy'. In the course of conversation he asked me directly, "What exactly do you look like?" I was a bit taken aback, but not knowing how else to answer, I said, "Well, I'm blonde, blue-eyed, and thin." He said, "Ahh, good!" At this point I got up the nerve to reciprocate in kind. "What do *you* look like", I inquired. "Oh, me?" he asked. "Well…I'm a cross between Jackie Gleason and Ernest Borgnine!" I laughed at this. What a great sense of humor! The next day my buzzer rang again, and I was told that my date was waiting downstairs in the lobby. Needless to say…I was actually greeted by a cross between Jackie Gleason and Ernest Borgnine. (But I think those actors were a lot *more* attractive than my date! And at least they were famous!) His personality was possibly even worse than his looks. The evening (slowly) passed, and so it was just another college experience!

Then there was the time that one of my friends asked if I'd like to join her with two of her visiting hometown guy-friends. They were going to a fabulous restaurant in Philly's Center City. Hey…fabulous restaurants were OK in my book! So, of course I said *yes*. There we were at the Pub Tiki, a wonderful Polynesian restaurant, and everyone was ordering everything. It was delicious. And then it happened. After ordering dessert, the guys told us to quickly go to the Ladies' Room, and after five minutes to meet them in the car. Their plan was to beat the check! I had become an unwitting criminal! I was mortified! But I was also kind of shy and definitely not confrontational, and so I did what I was told. As we sped away in that car, I was sure I was having a heart attack. We got away with it, but to this day, it really taught me a lesson: always check out the people you're having dinner with! (If anyone plans to turn me in, I'll just call this a piece of fiction! Creative license…you know!)

Here's another college story: Bill Cosby went to Temple University. I believe he had left a few years before I got there, but came back and graduated later. (I just Googled him and noticed that he has the same birthday as I do, and that he's six years my senior.) I remember that he had a crush on one of my friends, and I believe that he *did* ask her out. But the main conversation I recall was when he told me that he was going to go to New York to try to make it in show business. I said to my friends, "What is he *crazy* or something? He'll never make it!" (Don't ask me for stock tips either!)

Anyway, it's been fun reminiscing. They were great times, and I'll never forget them. I wonder if the kids today are having as much fun.

Girlfriends - (2010)

"Make new friends…but keep the old; one is silver, the other gold." That was a song I learned as a little girl in summer camp. So does that mean "old" friends are more golden than new ones? Not necessarily!

As an "only child" my girlfriends were extremely important to me. When I was 2 ½, I met the little girl who lived in the apartment right next door to ours. Our birthdays were exactly 1 month-to-the-day apart. (She's older!) We played Hide 'n' Seek, had sleepovers, and shared family occasions. When *we* moved to the suburbs, *her family* moved to the *same* suburbs. We both went to college in the same town, and we both married and had children (2 for me, 4 for her). And now, both in our 60s (she's *still* older), we see each other all the time, and we're still close. I met another of my current close friends in third grade. She kept hitting me over the head with her pen, but I've gotten over that by now. I'm still friendly with several of the "girls" I met in high school. And then there's my friend whom I met at my tennis club in my 40s. She and I could talk about *anything*…and we still do! Then there's my wonderful songwriting collaborator/friend; and then there are my college roommates who now live scattered in various cities all over the country. When we manage to get together, it's like we're still partying!

In my 50s, after a divorce and a new, wonderful second marriage, we moved into a gated community in the suburbs. I've made quite a few *new* friends. (My mom would've been so proud!) But after being here for almost 15 years, are they still *new*? Well, maybe new-*er*…but not necessarily *silver* as compared to *gold!* When you meet someone in your 50s or 60s, it's a very different experience from your childhood days. Each of us has been through what we've been through; sometimes divorce, sometimes widowhood, problems with grown kids, problems with money, aches and pains, and I could go on and on. But when you *do* connect…when you *do* click…there's something very special about bonding with a new friend.

We don't play Hide 'n' Seek; we don't have sleepovers, and we don't talk about boys; but we *do* go out to lunch, and we *do* talk on the phone, and we *do* go to dinners and parties with (or without) our men. If we're going through a difficult time, we help each other out. Or at least we try. We play tennis together, and best of all, we laugh together. I think maybe because we're the ages we are, we tend to open up sooner. Some are closer than others, but I feel very lucky to have so many new friends in my life.

So I think I'll quote the lyrics of another song: *"In good times, in bad times, I'll be on your side forever more! That's what friends are for!"*

HOT TUB FRIENDS IN FLORIDA - (2010)

So, there I am...sitting in the hot tub by the clubhouse pool at our Florida vacation home. This home, by the way, is one we bought seven years ago and had rented out for the last two years. We had been trying to sell it, but with the economy as it's been, we felt lucky to find renters. And now, the renters were gone, and so we bought our roundtrip tickets from New York to the West Palm Beach airport. We rented a car and drove twenty-five minutes to our home-away-from home. *Not!* I barely remembered where our bathrooms were...where we kept the dishes...or how to operate the washing machine. The renters had left the place in total disrepair, and it took about ten days to clean the oven, pull out the weeds from the patio, throw out the mould-filled towels, wipe down the counters, and dozens of other wonderful tasks nobody would ever want to do, especially on their vacation!

And did I forget to mention...upon our arrival in Florida, it was thirty-two degrees! THIRTY-TWO DEGREES! I think I had brought just two sweaters, lots of bathing suits, shorts, and T-shirts. We turned on the heat (once we remembered where the thermostat was) and sat down to watch TV in the living room. Of course, the living room TV did NOT work! Poor thing…it was totally dead. And…the cables leading to it had been nibbled by the dog owned by our renters! So, we bought a new TV. We HAD to in order to make our home "sell-able" according to our real estate broker…and we still *did* want to sell this house.

Finally, a day arrived that looked quite promising. The sun was shining; it was seventy degrees, and we decided to go to the clubhouse pool, just where I began this story. My husband and I couldn't find any unoccupied lounge chairs because the place was mobbed with visiting children and grandchildren. Now I have nothing against children – or grandchildren – I happen to have a few myself – but I really wanted a lounge chair. Oh well, we found two 'regular' chairs and sat down poolside. After swimming a few laps, I decided to go to the "spa" hot tub. I figured it would be good for my back. When I got there, I saw three little girls sitting around it. I smiled and said hello and got in the hot, bubbly water. That's when one of the girls said to me in a most wistful way…"I wish I were 14 so I could go in the hot tub". The other two girls agreed, and they pointed to the sign on the wall which, among other rules, stated that "NO ONE UNDER 14 IS ALLOWED IN THIS HOT TUB". So they sat on the edge, dangling their feet in the water. Then suddenly 3 young boys jumped in. They were yelling and laughing and pointing to their privates because their bathing suits were being puffed out in a funny way. Then 2 teenage boys literally splashed in, forming a minor tidal wave. So there we were – the nine of us – in the hot tub together. They started chatting, and being a friendly person, I joined their conversation. One of the younger kids asked me if I lived here all the time. I told him no, and that I lived in New York most of the year. He immediately said with enthusiasm, "Oh…do you know the Millers?" I explained that New York is pretty big, and there are lots of "Millers" there.

At this moment a woman in uniform angrily approached us and, directing her attention to me, said, "Anybody under 14 can NOT be in this pool!" I told her that I had never met these kids before in my life! She smiled at me, and then she made sure that the 'little' kids got out. That was when the 15-year-old started chatting with me about how excited he was that he was getting his driving permit in a couple of months when he turned 16. And then he was talking to his friend about a mutual friend of theirs who was caught smoking "weed". This really piqued my interest, and while being quite surprised to be in-cluded in this conversation, I asked him if a lot of his friends smoked marijuana. He said, "Oh yeah…*a lot!*" And then he told me that lots of kids his age took Oxycontin…and lots of them drank alcohol. He said he's also known some who have tried crack cocaine. He rattled this off so calmly, while I, on the other hand, was truly amazed and dumb-founded. We chatted for another ten minutes at which point I had had enough of the hot tub…AND teenagers! I must say, that although it was an eye-opener, it made me quite sad. Is this what our future gen-erations are all about?

We stayed in Florida for about two weeks, and soon it was time to pack our stuff and head back home to New York. Although we had social-ized quite a bit, played tennis and a little golf, I was ready! We returned our rental car and got to the airport on time. Our flight arrived almost an hour early, and we were home right away. The very next day we were hit by a blizzard with 18 inches of snow and very heavy winds.

Am I glad we're going back to Florida in a month? Do I wish our house would be sold? Well…*maybe*…and…*YES!* But I *do* look forward to going into that hot tub again! I hope my new friends will be waiting for me there. And I hope they're clean and sober! Maybe this could be a good lesson for us grown-ups; maybe we all need to have more con-versations with our *own* kids – and our new hot tub-friends – about the realities and dangers of drugs. As for me, I won't be silent next time. Who knew you had to be in a hot tub in Florida to find out what's *re-ally* going on with our youth today?

A DAY FOR THE BIRDS - (2011)

It started out like any other day. The weather in Long Island was sunny and bright…a perfect day for three women *of a certain age* (let's just say we're all AARP members!) to travel to the Big Apple for an early dinner and a Broadway show. The plan was to drive to the Syosset Railroad Station, take the 3:46 into Manhattan, walk to a lovely Italian restaurant for an early dinner, and then to a seven o'clock curtain on West 42nd Street. Sounds good…right?

Well, the *first* part was good…for *me!* We all went up to the ticket window, and my friend purchased her ticket with her credit card. It took quite a while…she was stipulating that she wanted a "round-trip, off-peak, Senior discount fare". When she finally got her ticket and signed the charge, it was my turn. Much like the woman in the movie "When Harry Met Sally", who witnessed Sally's (fake) orgasm right there in the coffee shop, I said, "I'll have what *she* just had." The ticket guy leaned in and looked at me and said, "But *she's* a Senior!" Yay!! Of course I told him that *I* was a Senior too…but like I said…*that* was good for *me!*

The good feeling lasted all of one minute. Upon leaving the ticket window we proceeded to walk up a large flight of stairs to the train platform. There we were…waiting for the train to New York with many other passengers. It was really crowded. The three of us were in deep conversation when all of a sudden, I felt a huge glob of what felt like a warm dollop of sour cream plop right onto my forehead! SPLAT! My hair was all wet, and my forehead was gooey. It took about twenty seconds for us all to realize what had just happened. Right above us, on a pipe that stretched along the entire length of the train platform… were three pigeons cackling away. I *know* they were laughing at me! I don't know why, because I have nothing against pigeons, though I *have* been known to enjoy a Cornish Hen every once in a while. Of course my "wonderful" friends started to get hysterical, and actually, so did I. We found some tissues and tried to wipe away the gook as best we could. And then the train arrived to take us to Manhattan. In reflection, I was truly thankful that I hadn't been yawning!

The trip was uneventful, although the train was so crowded, none of us could sit together, and I had the feeling that my seat-mate was a bit turned off by my wet pigeon-pooped hair, but I certainly had no intention of explaining myself to a busily- texting- teen. The restaurant was lovely. It was so early, we were the only patrons, but that was OK. And we certainly didn't mind when our waitress mistakenly brought us a second round of wine. We told her that we hadn't ordered it, but she insisted we have it. So what could we do? We drank it, and so we were having an even better time!

After dinner, we walked a couple blocks to the theatre. When we finally arrived, we climbed a few flights up to the third floor for our show, and we found our seats in the middle of Row K. Two minutes into the show, one of my friends had an unbelievable coughing fit. Not just a couple of "ahems"…mind you. It was an unending series of loud coughs…so loud that people started turning around to see what the disturbance was. At this point, she got up from her seat and told us she'd be in the lobby. We totally understood. However, an hour and a half later, with the first act still going strong, our friend had not returned to her seat. My other friend and I kept looking at each other, shrugging our shoulders with worry, and straining our necks around trying to locate our coughing pal. She was nowhere to be seen. Meanwhile, I was definitely not *into* the show. Maybe it was all the distractions…maybe it was the residual poop situation…but I was not having a great time.

Finally, it was Intermission! We found our friend in the lobby, and she informed us that she was going to go home because she just couldn't stop coughing in that theatre. We both responded immediately by saying that we wouldn't let her go alone…that we would leave as well. I said that I wasn't *loving* the show anyway, which was true. (It was "in previews", and when it's finally reviewed, it'll probably be the hottest show on Broadway...the one *we* walked out on! Oh well!) Once we decided to leave, we started to walk briskly to Penn Station to take a train home.

We arrived at Penn Station one minute too late for our train. So now we had to wait forty minutes for the next one. Penn Station is amazing at night. Here's how it works: Hundreds of people stand around waiting to find out what track their train will be on. All you know is that you're taking the 9:15 to Syosset. The track number will be announced when the train comes into the station. When the track number starts flashing, these hundreds of people converge – much like a cattle call – to the gate. You could lose your life doing this, but everyone seems to do it every day, so I guess it's basically safe.

Track 21...Track 21! We were pushed by the crowd to the gate and down the steps to our train. We luckily found an end seat with another facing it, so the three of us could actually sit together. There was a gentleman sitting there already, but he seemed friendly enough, so we squeezed in, knees butting against each other's knees, but together! I just couldn't get past the fact, however, that this gentleman was a dead ringer for Alex Trebek of "Jeopardy". I suddenly felt the need to say everything in question form. At this point my friends and I became so giddy from all of our little experiences, that we just couldn't stop laughing. I mean REALLY LAUGHING. Poor Alex. He must have thought we were laughing at *him*. We actually tried to explain *why* we were laughing, but we were laughing too hard to talk or explain.

We finally made it home from our little adventure. And now...here's the FINAL JEOPARDY ANSWER:

"Before the advent of cars, one could see and smell the emissions of horse-drawn wagons in New York. They served to nourish a large population of English sparrows. People used *this expression* to politely say that the subject matter is worthless or just a bunch of horse crap."

FINAL JEOPARDY QUESTION: "What is... *For the birds?*"

Our big day certainly wasn't worthless...but in a certain sense...it *was absolutely* "for the birds"!

MY 50ᵀᴴ HIGH SCHOOL REUNION - (2011)

I recently went to my 50th High School Reunion. I had gone to High School in a New York City suburb called Lawrence on the south shore of Long Island. The Class of 1961 – about 425 students – was composed of a mixture of religions, races, and economic backgrounds.

My High School years were pretty good. The teachers were excellent; some of them quite strict (like Mademoiselle Benson for French...*ooh la la* - she scared me half to death!), but most of them interesting and caring. I was a pretty good student, and so I got good marks, was on the Honor Roll, and did OK on my SATs. I was friendly with the "popular girls", but somehow, I never quite made it with the "popular boys". I was skinny, shy, and small-breasted (still am!), and except for one boy, I never felt like I was in the "In" group. As a matter of fact, when I first got to college (Temple University in Philadelphia), I was absolutely amazed that lots of boys were asking me out! Wow! Maybe it was something in the water there! What I *really* think is that I finally came to like *myself!* I realized I was attractive, funny, and smart...if I say so myself! I ultimately got married, had 2 kids, got divorced 28 years later, found new love, and got married again.

And so now it was time for my 50th High School Reunion. Ginger, a very close friend of mine, whom I've known since we were 2, was organizing the reunion, and I was very happy to help her with my computer skills, my contacts, and anything else she might need. About a year before the scheduled event in October, 2011, Ginger booked the

Lawrence Golf Club for the big day, and we started compiling spread sheets of all our classmates so that we could hand out directories at the event. This was no easy feat. There were other alumni Ginger had helping her as well, from all different states and cities; they were almost like detectives trying to find the whereabouts of various classmates with whom we had lost touch.

I must have driven to Ginger's home (about a 45-minute drive) more than 6 or 7 times…specifically for reunion business. We'd meet for lunch, and then…we'd get down to work! She would read me the information she had accumulated on her hundreds of post-its, and I would add the info onto the spreadsheets. During this process, we had a million laughs; some recalling various 'kids', some because I made some really funny typos, and some just because we were having so much fun thinking about how our reunion would actually be!

As the time drew closer to the event, and our classmates' checks started coming in the mail, we found a DJ; we located a photographer; and we had our directories printed up. We also had to plan a menu with the caterer. We handled it all! (Of course it was a bit unsettling to learn that two weeks before our event, there was a huge fire in the kitchen of the Club, and the firemen had to break through the roof! But the caterer assured Ginger that our party would go on! Phew! How could we ever have contacted *everyone* – from New York to Florida to Copenhagen to *wherever* – in time to tell them about a new venue!)

And now the day was here! My husband and I arrived at 6:00 PM, an hour early as planned. He - and the husband of a close friend of mine from our class - would be signing in all our classmates. That friend, Bean (real name "Nancy"…too long a story which goes back to grade school; anyway, Nancy became "Bean") and I went immediately to the bar. (How else to gear oneself up upon the prospect of seeing people you haven't seen in 50 years?) So, with my Pinot Grigio in hand, I was ready!

And they started to arrive. On Facebook and Twitter they might say OMG, but at age 68 I don't really say that, but that's exactly how I felt! Wow! What a surge of adrenaline as my classmates entered the building! Everyone was wearing a name tag sticker which had our individual yearbook pictures on it. So as I was hugging each new person, I would check out their name tag so I would know who it was. Of course I wasn't wearing my trusty reading glasses at the time, so there was a lot of squinting going on from my end! I have a feeling that some of the "boys" might have thought I was winking at them; but I wasn't! I was just trying to figure out who this white haired older man was (who used to have wavy black hair)! And anyway, I did that with the women too!

After the hors d'oeuvres by the bar, we all went into the ballroom. The DJ started playing Elvis and Dion and Chuck Berry and others. I don't think I ever sat down! All the "girls" were dancing together and having a blast! Some of the guys were up there too! Then I heard Chubby Checkers say, "Come on everybody…I'm gonna sing my song and it won't take long! We're gonna do the Twist, and it goes like this!" And so we twisted the night away! Just writing about it now gives me goose bumps. It was – in current lingo – truly AWESOME! We also did some group dances – maybe 50 people were up there dancing – and everyone was smiling!

A photographer took a group photo of all the classmates, as well as mini-group photos of grade school alumni. The buffet was lovely, though I hardly remember what I ate – or *if* I ate! We danced some more, and we reminisced even more. And then it was over. We hugged, and we kissed, and we promised to keep in touch. Maybe that will happen. I hope so.

I received the group photo in today's mail. What a happy crowd! I don't know if there will ever be a 60th, and I'm not even sure if I'd want one, but our 50th High School Reunion was one for the books! A definite "Best Seller"

Mayo On The Side! - (2012)

No…this is not a new culinary delight; this is what happened to me the other day at lunch…really. It was after I played tennis in my indoor tennis league in Jericho. Several of the women enjoy lunch together at a local coffee shop. We all get along, and the conversation is always interesting.

So that day, instead of having my "regular" quiche, salad, and iced tea special, I ordered a BLT on whole wheat with mayonnaise on the side. Reasonable…right? I *thought* so!

Well, the service was not exactly the best that day. The place was pretty crowded; lots of women and even a few tables filled with men. When the waitress finally headed our way, carrying five plates at a time (how do they do that?), I was hungry and ready! The woman opposite me got her huge Caesar salad with chicken on top; the one next to her got her grilled cheese with (very, very crisp) bacon on top; and three other women were served various and sundry salads. Now it was *my* turn! As the waitress approached my corner of the table, she kind of bumped into something – or just took a tiny misstep – and the plate carrying my BLT, etc. kind of jiggled in the air. She actually caught it, but on the way the small round container of mayonnaise (on the side) flipped out…and landed – BOOM! – right into my pocketbook, which was hanging on the side of my chair! Let me clarify that: it landed right into the *little pocket* in my pocketbook which holds my cell phone! No mayonnaise got anywhere else but IN and SURROUNDING my cell phone!

"Oh My Gosh!" said the waitress and everyone else at the table, including *me!* I grabbed for my phone, pulled it out of my bag, and it was covered from head to toe – or screen to keyboard – in white, gooey mayonnaise! The waitress was extremely upset, and I felt bad for her, so I tried to remain cool. She ran and got me a towelette to wipe it down with…and so I wiped it down. I kept saying, "It's ok…it's ok…it'll be fine!" And actually…it *was!*

And so I leave you with two simple warnings: 1) Make sure your pocketbook is zipped close when you are at a restaurant, and 2) Never order mayonnaise on the side!

3

Gizmos, Gadgets, and Botox

The "Other Woman"

Don't look too closely; I'm better from afar...or from the back!

I'M GIVING TiVo THE HEAVE-HO - (2008)

We recently received a TiVo as a gift. In case you're not yet familiar with this phenomenon, let me explain. TiVo is sort of like a VCR, but a lot more advanced. It's a contraption which attaches to your TV or cable box and allows you to digitally record your favorite shows for the rest of your life. You don't even have to tell it when the shows are on; it knows. It will also record other shows, similar to ones you might request, just because it *thinks* you might like them. It also has the ability to pause and reverse a live program. Don't ask how…it just does. Now believe me, this was a lovely, thoughtful, and expensive gift. It's just driving me crazy…that's all! We had recently ordered Digital Cable, and when the cable guys came to our house to install the boxes, we told them we'd 'show our appreciation' if they'd hook up our TiVo. Thank goodness, because all those wires and inputs and outputs looked a lot like NASA to me.

When I was five, my parents bought a Castro Convertible Sofa, and they couldn't figure out how to open it. I could, and I did. I once put together a complete gas barbecue grill. I'm the one who knows how to program the VCRs; I'm the only one who can re-set the time on the answering machines and the heat thermostats. I'm by no means electronically challenged. But I think I met my match with TiVo.

Once the TiVo was installed, we *thought* it was working correctly. However, our first clue that something was amiss was the fact that our TiVo remote wasn't able to turn on the set. So now we're looking at 4 different remotes on our coffee table: the TV remote, the cable remote, the DVD remote, and the TiVo remote. We didn't *remotely* know what to do with *any* of them, but after reading through the two textbook-like manuals, which came with our TiVo, I had the feeling that *all* we should need is our TiVo remote.

I tried to follow the prompts, but promptly got confused, so I called their 800 number. This is where I kind of lost it. I'm now on the phone having a conversation with a tape recording. Really. The recorded female voice is saying, "It seems like you have a problem! If you do, say YES!" "Yes", I say. "I didn't hear that", says the voice. "YES!" I scream. "Good", she says. "Now tell me what it is." And then she proceeds to list a series of potential problems none of which was mine. "Which one is it?" she repeats. (She's starting to get on my nerves now.) When I answered in a complete sentence, she interrupted me. "I didn't get that," she said, which stunned me into silence. And then I heard something I had been hoping for. On her list of possibilities, she said, "If you'd like a live agent…say *live agent!*" "LIVE AGENT!" I screamed. And then…after a pause…a *recorded* male voice came on the line and told me that if I want to speak to a live agent, I should dial a different number. He also informed me that I might have to wait up to 15 or 20 minutes until my call was taken. This was after an hour of my time in the first place. I think I screamed something like "Thanks for nothing, pal!" and then I hung up. And I'm the same person my daughter criticizes for being too nice to everyone! Though I felt much better, I still couldn't turn my TV set on.

This story has a happy ending. I calmed down, and about an hour later I dialed the original number again. By some miraculous twist of fate, I was able to follow the instructions of the recorded lady, if you could call her that, and I got the TiVo remote to actually work. It's been one week since then, and it's still working, and I'm still learning the myriad of things I can do with this machine. It's truly amazing. But if I ever happen to meet that lady in person, I hope I don't slap her. And if there are any other technical problems that come up, well, sorry but it'll be heave-ho to the TiVo! Did you get *that*, lady?

CYBER HELL - (2009)*

Two weeks ago my computer died. Just think: All my stories (I'm a writer)…All my songs (I'm a lyricist)…All my poems (I write Candle Lighting poems for Bar Mitzvahs and Sweet 16s)…All the email addresses of everyone in my life…All my photos (kids, grandkids, don't ask!) Gone, gone, gone! In one bright flash with a corresponding buzz, my computer/internet work of over the last ten years was reduced to a totally black screen. I couldn't even see the mouse's arrow; no hour glass to wait for. My mind couldn't comprehend what my eyes were actually seeing. How could I have become so dependent on this machine? Well, I don't really know…but I was! (Is there such a thing as "Sui-cybe" or killing oneself over computer problems?)

The next question was: who do I call? Well, my first call went to my "Internet Provider". These are the same people who "provide" our cable as well as our phones. After listening to their recorded tape of what number to press for which problem, and that there might be a 20-minute wait, I pressed and waited. When a human finally came on the line, and my account number, my address, and my secret password were ascertained, I was assured that the problem was with the *computer*… not the *provider*. So now I had to call the computer company.

At this point, it was 2:00 PM on a Saturday. I'm revealing that detail because I didn't hang up the phone with them until 8:10 PM! Not to mention that I spent another three hours with this company on the following day! That's longer than some marriages! Anyway, when I first called the 800 number, I was greeted by the usual recorded messages. But this time it was my job to speak to the recorded voice: "Is this problem concerning a home computer? A home-business computer? A business computer?" "A home computer", I replied. "What? I didn't get that", said the voice. "A HOME COMPUTER", I screamed. She still didn't get that. I remained silent (with fury) for a minute or so, and then I heard, "Please stay on the line and one of our agents will assist you." And shortly thereafter Deepan was saying to me, "How can I help you?"

Well, it turned out that Deepan *couldn't* help me. My "problem" was beyond the free-800 phone call-help; I needed to be connected to a *computer-expert-with-a-fee* ($250 for a one-year service plan!) so he could remotely operate my computer and uncover the problem for me. What else could I do? So I said "OK". But this was not as easy as it sounded. After waiting on hold again – this time for 15 minutes – Rajeev came on the line. I explained the situation, and Rajeev proceeded to tell me what to do so that he would be able to operate my computer from his end (that would be in India). It involved a lot of pressing and holding the on-off button while continuously pressing the F8 key on the keyboard. Hold…press, press. Hold…press, press. Suddenly a new screen popped up with all kinds of white text and strange symbols. After highlighting, pressing Enter, highlighting again, etc. (this activity went on for about an hour and a half), I was finally able to click a button that accepted Rajeev to take the controls of my computer. *YES…I ACCEPT! JUST DO IT!!!*

For the next four hours Rajeev was doing his thing. Luckily, I was able to put my phone on "speaker" and lay it down on my desk; otherwise my ear would have become numb, and my arm would have been broken. I was put on 'hold' maybe six different times – with loud music filling the airwaves; the longest time I was on 'hold' was 32 minutes; I timed it! Finally…and I mean finally…Rajeev told me that the job was done. He said that he had retrieved my files and that I needed to buy a new anti-virus program so this problem would never happen again. He said he could install that for me now, and that he would send me the actual disk and information by UPS. Once again I said "OK", and I gave him my credit card number again so that I could be charged an additional $89 for the anti-virus. Well, I HAD to…right?

Turns out: WRONG! The next day, when my computer wasn't functioning right, guess who I called. You got it! (I knew the number by heart at this point.) After waiting and pressing buttons (I won't go into it again!), I reached a new representative. I gave her the whole sad story…and…guess what? My computer did not have enough memory to support the new anti-virus which her colleague had installed. So she un-installed it. It only took three hours. Meanwhile, what about the $250 and the $89 I had just shelled out? Well, she told me that they would refund $200 of the $250 because after all, their representative had spent a lot of time on this. *Oh really?* As for the $89 for the anti-virus package, she explained that when I received this package by UPS (it was too late to stop it from coming), I should then send it back to them and my $89 will be credited on my card. They were going to email me the proper label, and if I used that and brought it to a UPS store, then it would cost me nothing to ship it. After several failed tries, the label finally came through, and I printed it out. The package arrived, and I brought it and the new label to my local UPS store. The UPS lady told me that in order to ship it, I needed a certain kind of box to ship it in. So I bought it for $4.50. Hey…it was a bargain! I only lost almost two full exhausting days of my life, and it only cost me $54.50!

Unfortunately, the story doesn't end there. The next day, when I dared to go onto my computer, I saw that not everything was restored. I was still missing every email address I ever had. Friends, relatives, business people…who cares! Big deal! Well it WAS a big deal! Luckily, a friend of mine had recommended a "computer-person" who lived nearby. I called her; she came over; and in a little more than one hour, she "fixed" my computer! And she installed a new anti-virus-protection… for free! Of course, everything runs a bit differently, but I'm learning more and more about it every day.

This is the first story I've written on my computer since this whole mis-adventure started. I think I needed to do that, and I feel better already. And I know – if this ever should happen again – what NOT to do! And now so do *you!*

* By the way…the same thing happened again in 2013! Don't ask!!!

CAN'T STAND LOOKING AT MYSELF
WITH MY READING GLASSES ON! - (2010)

When did this happen to me? I used to be somewhat attractive. At least that's what people told me. I also used to be able to read a book or the newspaper without having to locate my reading glasses. And if I don't have my reading glasses on, sometimes it's hard to find them! (Especially when they're on my head!) What a predicament!

So, the other day, I put down the book I was reading – actually it's not a "book", it's my Kindle (I might be a Senior, but I'm right up there with all the modern technology!) – and went to the mirror to put on my make-up. With my glasses still on, I hardly recognized myself. My face kind of reminded me of a roadmap from Google, only missing that little red icon with the letter 'A' saying "you are here"! Well, I didn't want to be 'here'! Just to check things out, I removed my glasses and looked again. Much better! But then I realized that if I wanted people to think I'm still attractive, then I have to hang out with only those who had vision problems, and that would definitely leave out my grown kids and my adorable grandkids. Therefore, I would have to deal with this situation. But how?

I had been reading and hearing a lot about Botox. One of my friends was going to do it, and so I thought I would too. The 'Board Certified Dermatologist' actually made house calls, and so my friend and I set up an appointment to get Botoxed together right in our kitchens. (In retrospect, I got the feeling that in truth he was actually a 'BORED Certified Dermatologist', but that's a whole other story!) The nice doctor carefully injected a few places on my forehead…in those deep frown lines…and that was that. The problem was…that WASN'T that! The next day I woke up, and the frown lines were reduced, but my eyelids were drooping over my eyes so that I could barely see. And I couldn't even lift the brows – like you do when you're surprised – because that part of my forehead was basically paralyzed! My only thought was, "Thank goodness Botox only lasts a few months!" Well, it finally wore off, and I could once again look surprised. The lids, however, never quite regained my original non-droopy look. Oh well.

Now, back to coping with my image as seen through my reading glasses. I went out and purchased a bunch of very expensive creams - some for daytime, some for night - but the wrinkles weren't reduced nearly as much as my bank account. Lately, I've tried to be philosophical about the whole thing; as long as I have my health…that's what really matters. But then again, parts of my body hurt which never ever hurt before; my back, my neck, my arms, and my hands. Maybe I left something out, but I keep forgetting exactly what. That's another thing. How many times have I walked into a specific room in my house and forgotten what I was looking for? But, unfortunately, I always seem to remember to look in the mirror.

I guess the answer is to be more accepting of myself. What I *look* like is NOT who I am! I have a husband, children, grandchildren, and friends who love me. That's pretty special. And as I bask in the glow of their love and caring, I think maybe I AM still pretty! Who knew a Google roadmap could be so beautiful!

Don't look too closely!

I THINK HE'S CHEATING ON ME! - (2010)

I'm not positive, but something's definitely going on. He tells me he loves me, but a woman *knows* when something's wrong. We've *both* been married before – each of us for quite some time – and we both left those marriages. We lived together for 12 years and got married a year and a half ago. We've been known in our community as *"The Romantic Couple"*…and we *were!* He used to hold my hand all the time, but now he can't seem to take his hands off *her.* And I think I even know her name. It's kind of a nickname/first name…kind of stupid, if you ask *me*. It's like the silly nicknames of a couple of women I once knew; names like *Cookie*…and *Peaches!* Ridiculous…right?

OK…so I did a little snooping, and I found out that this one's nickname is "Blackberry". Can you believe *that* one! You might say, "What are you talking about? That's a *phone!!* Well OK…sure, in your dreams it *might* be a phone, but I just *know* it's another woman! He's *always* turning her on…I'm sure of it! I can just see his fingers moving lightly all over her. I bet he can't stop looking at her; I think he often whispers in her ear and writes her little love notes with his *thumbs…how kinky!* He responds to any little sound she makes…and she makes a *lot* of sounds. One time I overheard him talking to a friend about putting her on "vibrate". I was really surprised because he never was much into that sort of thing with *me*. I think I might have actually walked in on him right after they were making love! I could swear I heard the song "The Entertainer" blasting away! How can I ever compete with *that?* (And *please*, don't tell me it was a *ringtone!*)

And another thing: I suspect she's very young. I think she's wearing him down. Ever since I've become aware of *"Ms." Blackberry*, I've noticed that my man is kind of hunched over. "It's just a *PHONE*", you might say again. "Everyone who has that kind of cell phone is *always* leaning over towards it. They're trying to find out – every minute of every day – exactly *who* is calling…or *who* is emailing them". Now I ask you…is it really so important to be up-to-the-minute on which five dollar sub at Subway is on special this week? Or that Classmates.com wants him to register on their site? He tells me, "It's *business!*" Yeah right!

I know the kind of "business" you're talking about, mister! FUNNY BUSINESS! MONKEY BUSINESS! I wasn't born yesterday

Nah…it can't be just a phone! I think maybe – like that movie said - he's *just not that into me* anymore. So now I've got to figure out just how to get him back. I could come up with my own nickname…maybe something like *Strawberry!* Yeah…I like that…*Strawberry!* And you know that "thumb" thing might be a whole new sensation. I could get *into* that! I could start to make all kinds of sounds! How's *this? Ooh! Ahh!* I could even try to beep if he wanted me to. You know, like *beep-beep-beep* for faster; *beeeeeep* for slower. This could work!

If he still insists that he's *not* cheating…and it's really *just* his phone, then I will say, "OK, darling. I believe you." But between you and me, I knew the truth all along: it was definitely another woman, but, you know…I still want him back. And then I will have him all to myself. Our life will be *so* sweet…like a great big hot fudge sundae…with a *Strawberry* on top!

FOOL ME TWICE? - (2011)

As former President George W. Bush said, "Fool me once…uh…shame on you! Ya fool me…uh…you can't get fooled again!" Unfortunately, *I* was fooled twice…but not by anyone else but *me!* It's really kind of unfortunate when you spend what you consider a lot of money - to hopefully look a little better - and then it turns out that you look ten times worse!! That's what happened to me!

It's hard to admit, but, here goes…I'm a Senior! And what's more…I'm *proud* to be a Senior. I still play tennis; I go to the gym from time to time; and my husband and I have many romantic evenings together… at restaurants and even when we get back home! But I AM a mother of 2 almost-middle-aged kids, and a grandmother (so far) to 3 boys, aged from 1 to 9 years. I am a writer (of stories such as this) and a lyricist of hundreds of songs…some of which were actually recorded and released on various labels by various performers.

If you've been following my stories, you know that a little over a year ago, we were planning a big dinner party, and I decided that I'd try a little Botox. Hey…what's wrong with getting rid of those annoying frown lines? Everybody else was doing it. Why shouldn't I? Well, a friend and I found a "board certified dermatologist" right in our gated condo community, and so one day he came to her kitchen and injected both of us. Easy…right? Well…not so easy. SHE looked great! Good for her! *I*, on the other hand, had a droopy right eye. Who cared about frown lines when my eye lid was drooping down? I guess I could have said – as the song goes – "It's my party, and I'll cry if I want to…You would cry too - if it happened to you!" But I went bravely on and actually somehow managed to survive and have a good time at our party!

Of course I thought, "I'll never do *that* again! No Botox for *this* gal… ever again!" And now, a year and a half later, looking at another friend's forehead and seeing that she really looked great, I thought, "Gee, maybe it was a fluke back then! Maybe it was the *doctor*…not the Botox!" So, I found out the name of *this* doctor and made an appointment. He was a very lovely, intelligent, and understanding man who listened to my droopy tale of woe. He informed me that, unfortunately, maybe 2 out of 100 patients do, in fact, develop the "droops"…but…that it was extremely rare. I thought…what the heck…let's GO for it! And so I gave Botox a second chance.

I met two other friends for lunch the next day, and I shared my recent experience with them. They both thought I looked terrific! YAY! But then, twenty-four hours later, BOTH my eyelids started to droop…big time! And…if anyone wanted to surprise me…with ANYTHING… they'd never know I was surprised because I could not raise my eyebrows! I actually called the doctor, and he was totally receptive and saw me that afternoon. He looked terribly disappointed (I almost felt bad for him), and he gave me one extra shot in the hopes of helping with the droops. He told me that things would probably improve in a couple of weeks. I hope so. And now it's several weeks later. If you had never met me before, I'm not sure if you would notice anything. But if you knew me, you'd probably ask me what was wrong…because you'd think I was dozing off or something!

So…I was fooled twice! But the good news is…I'm really OK. Hey… you gotta try things sometimes…even twice…right? Just think, when the Botox wears off, I might look just as good as I did two months ago! And although I think it's really great for SOME people…YOU JUST CAN'T FOOL ME THREE TIMES!

4

Kids

My three grandsons at Halloween in 2013

Anjelica and Jancy teaching me how to
take a picture with my iphone…DUH…

What's A Grandma? -(2007)

Webster defines the word "grandmother" as follows: "The mother of one's father or mother; also called *grandam*." Then I went a step further and looked up *"grandam"*, and that definition was *"Old Woman, from the French"*. I wasn't thrilled with Mr. Webster at this point!

Here are some other thoughts on the subject, which I found on the Internet. They were collected from a kindergarten class. *"A Grandmother is a lady who has no little children of her own. She likes other people's."* And *"Everybody should try to have a Grandmother, especially if you don't have television, because they are the only grownups who like to spend time with us. When they take us for walks, they slow down past things like pretty leaves and caterpillars."*

I have two grandsons so far: Jake, who just turned 5, and Davis, who turned 1 in September. They are adorable, and I love them dearly. But I can't believe what a "Nervous Nellie" I've become at certain times when they are in my care! Sometimes I wonder how I *ever* raised my daughter and son without the anxiety I feel now as a Grandma. I was cool, calm, and collected. I was also young!

One time, several years ago, Jake had a 'sleepover' at my house. All of a sudden, he was crying and boiling hot. He was fine when he had arrived, but now he definitely had a fever. And I didn't have any Children's Tylenol. Larry was out of town on a business trip, and so I had to maneuver a screaming, flailing Jake into the car seat, and I managed to get the Tylenol from the local Seven/Eleven. Phew! Jake was a lot better in the morning, but I didn't sleep for one minute! *That* was scary!

And then there was the time recently that Davis was recovering from surgery and had stitches in his head. I was sitting with them in their playroom, and I watched as Jake picked up a toy golf club and began to swing like Tiger Woods. I think I was having a heart attack! I was so nervous that Jake would accidentally hit Davis right in the head! My daughter, however, calmly inserted herself between the two boys, and the danger was averted.

And now I want to illustrate how very smart my grandson, Jake, is. When he was visiting me a couple years ago (he was 4), he invited me to accompany him to the bathroom. So, as he was sitting, doing his business, with great concentration, he asked me, "Grandma, how old are you?" I replied, "How old do you *think* I am, Jake?" He thought about it for a while and said, "Well, my Mom is 35". He looked at me and said, "So…are you 36?" I *told* you…He's a *genius!*

Halloween Stories - (2009)

Halloween is always fun in our gated community on Long Island. I love the idea of putting those little "pumpkin signs" up on our garage doors so the kids know which doorbells are OK to ring. We stocked up on – as the kids say – *awesome* candy this year: Kit Kats, Hershey Bars, Gummy Bears, Butter Fingers, and Nestle Crunch! You can't beat that combo! So, on Saturday, October 31st in the afternoon, we were more than ready. We put our sign up and waited.

At about 3:15 the first bell rang. Larry and I both ran to the door with our big bowls of candy, and there, before us, were five boys…maybe 11 or 12 years old…in T-shirts and jeans carrying Shoprite bags. "Trick or Treat!" they yelled. I held out the bowl to them, but feeling rather gypped about the lack of any costumes, I said, "So…what are your costumes today?" One said, with a total straight face, "T-shirt and jeans!" Another said, "Me too…but I have a really cool mask!" which he then took out of his pocket to show me. Oh yeah…*cool…I guess.* A third volunteered, "I'm goin' as my cousin…and he's goin' as me…and the other guy is just goin' as a 12-year-old!" After they each grabbed fistfulls of candy, they asked if there was any more inside! Uh…not *really!* (The funniest was when Larry asked them which condo they were from. The answer: Brooklyn! Guess they were visiting their Long Island cousin!)

Of course there followed many fabulous princesses, soldiers, fairies, bunny rabbits, and Power Rangers too; there were triplets in costumes too adorable for words!

But this is not quite the Halloween I remember from my youth! When I was a little girl, growing up on the South Shore of Long Island, I remember creating fabulous costumes, going Trick or Treating with my little neighbor friends, and getting tons of treats! Candy, raisins, nuts, cookies, sometimes even money! It was great! We also used to carry chalk – and some kids even carried eggs – just in case people didn't give us our treats! (I, of course, never had to go that route!)

One thing I *do* remember, which I feel I must admit right here, is that the day after Halloween, I became quite the 9-year-old entrepreneur! I set up a stand on the corner of my street, and yes…I sold my candy at a discount! And people actually bought it! Of course the truth is…my mother was my biggest customer!

So…I guess I really can't complain about this year's Halloween's shenanigans. After all, I never saw any candy stands at the clubhouse the next day. And there were no chalk marks or eggs on my driveway! Phew!

DAVIS AND THE WATER BOTTLE - (2009)

I was in Battery Park – downtown New York City – playing with my 3-year-old grandson, Davis. So I take the cap off of a bottle of water for him, and he grabs the blue cap with a mischievous look in his eyes, and he says, "Grandma…heth a tahth?" Baffled, I looked at him quizzically, and said, "What, Davis? What are you saying?" "HETH A TAHTH…HETH A TAHTH!!" he repeated. And then it hit me! He was saying "Heads or Tails?" (What did it matter that the blue cap was exactly the same on both sides!) "Oh…I see! I get it! OK…*Heads!*" And so Davis threw the water bottle cap way up in the air. It finally landed, and he quickly picked it up. I asked, "Did I win?" He looked at it very carefully…and then up at me sadly.

"TAHTH…YOU LOOTHE!!! So sad…but also funny!

Nakiyah - (2010)

Nakiyah! (Pronounced Na-*KYE*-uh) What an unusual name! That's what I thought when I first heard it. It was the name of the nine-year-old little girl I was about to mentor. I had been volunteering as a mentor for the past decade at a local elementary school. The first few years my "mentees" (a weird word…right?) were two sisters, ages 9 and 10, Maribel and Joana. When they went off to middle school, I started with Nancy. Each of these girls presented different challenges, and I like to think that I helped them with their school work and maybe even got them to think about life just a bit differently…in a good way with higher hopes in their futures. And then Nancy went on to the middle school. I keep in touch with all three, and they seem to be doing quite well.

So at the beginning of the school season I was ready to meet my new charge. The helpful social worker and one of the teachers at the elementary school suggested Nakiyah. I believe they thought she could use a little extra attention. Well, I had no idea what was in store for me! Nakiyah is an attractive, thin, almost-as-tall-as-me (5'4") amazingly active little girl. She doesn't walk; she trots. She doesn't chuckle; she roars. She doesn't necessarily want to do homework; she wants to do whatever she wants to do! She knows all the cultural slang of 2010. And she uses it on me!

Just for the record, I have two married adult children and (so far) two adorable grandsons, ages 7 and 3 ½. Now I'm no "spring chicken", but I've always been told I have a youthful look about me. Well, I don't think Nakiyah thinks so. I was trying to have a conversation with her about I-don't-know-what, when she got up from her chair, put her hands on her hips, and with a whole lot of attitude said, "*Woman…* how old are you?" Stammering, I said, "I'm…uh…in my…uh…60s. Why do you want to know?" "*Woman*…I just do! And *woman*…you are *old, old, old!*" So I answered her in kind, "*Woman*…that's not very nice…and it's not even *true!*" At this point Nakiyah stood up, put her hands exasperatedly up in the air and told me with even more attitude, "*YOU* can't say "*woman*" like that!" "Why not?" said I. And she pinched her wrist and then she pinched mine and answered, "Because I'm this…and you're that!" meaning *'she's* African American…and I'm *not!'* Try to get spelling homework done in *that* atmosphere!

So instead of just doing homework, Nakiyah and I have gotten into the routine of having all kinds of conversations for our hour-and-a-half together once a week. I know that she lives with her "Nanny", who is actually her Great-Grandmother. Nanny seems to be quite strict, but also very caring and protective. (Nakiyah says SHE'S *old, old, old* too… just like *me!* Comforting…isn't it?) Nakiyah has a younger brother who lives in another town with another relative. When she had her 10th birthday, I brought cupcakes and pretzels (her favorite) and a couple of gifts which I thought she'd like. Although she actually had requested an Ipod Touch (which is a whole lot of money), I gave her a cute pair of earrings (her ears are pierced). I think she was happy.

Sometimes she challenges my intelligence. One day, as we were sitting down at our desk in the school library, she stood up, put her hands on her hips, and with a swagger of her head said, "O.K, Ms. Carole…

spell *vicissitude!*" Luckily, I *could!* A bit taken aback, but nevertheless still challenging, she ordered, "Now spell *pulchritude!*" Again, luckily, I *did!* I then asked her if she knew the meanings of these words. She didn't...and so I told her their meanings. But I was truly impressed by the research she had done just to stump me.

It's really a good thing that I have a pretty decent sense of self because 'hanging' with Nakiyah could make a person lose all their confidence. One day, as we were engrossed in conversation, she stopped talking and started looking at me in a strange way. I asked, "What's the matter?" She pointed to my neck. "What's that?" she asked as though something was crawling on me. Being the age I am, I immediately held my head up - which usually smoothes that area - and replied, "It's my neck! What did you *think* it was?" "It's a *Lizard Neck*", she said. Well... my neck might not be what it used to be, but it's no *Lizard Neck*... OK? And I wasn't going to have any more of *that* conversation. I let her know that although she was trying to be funny, certain words can hurt a person's feelings...and that what she said wasn't nice. I believe that this was quite a learning experience for Nakiyah, and I think she understood what I was saying.

As an aside, let me mention that when I started mentoring Nakiyah, I had been living with a wonderful man named Larry for the past 11 years. My previous marriage of 28 years had ended with divorce, and I was very happy in my situation. Larry and I decided quite recently to 'seal the deal' and get married. We were very much in love and decided that a wedding would be a very happy event for us and all our friends and family...and that we wanted to share our happiness. During one of our mentoring sessions, I told Nakiyah that I was going to get married. Well, she immediately stood up and paced the room...back and forth... back and forth. "What's the matter?" I asked. She shook her head with exasperation and said, "I need to write this Larry-guy a note!" And she sat down at the desk and began writing in her notebook, but she was covering up whatever she was writing so I couldn't possibly see it. She looked up at me and ordered, "Do not read this till you leave here!" When I got in my car, I opened up the folded notebook paper and read the following in her very precise handwriting:

> "Dear Larry, if you ever mistreat Ms. Carole, you will have to meet me in a dark alley.
>
> Nakiyah."

So I guess she likes me!

And I have grown to really like *her*. During a recent session in June, we were told that it was to be our last one for the year because the after-school activities were over, and there would be no more late bus for the children. I spoke with the social worker and we wrote up a permission slip for Nakiyah to take home to Nanny. If she signed it, it would al-low me to have a "date" with Nakiyah during the summer season to take her out to lunch…or to an animal farm…or to a fish pond near where I live so we could feed the fish…but mainly to strengthen our relationship and keep it going so we can resume the mentoring next year in fifth grade. In speaking to the social worker on the phone later that week, it seemed that Nanny was not in favor of signing the permission slip. Nakiyah was disappointed, and so was I. But the social worker suggested that Nakiyah and I could actually share a lunch hour together in her office…and so a date was made for the following Wednesday.

I arrived at 12:15, and five minutes later a beaming Nakiyah ran in and hugged me so hard, I thought she'd break my (lizard) neck! She was so happy to see me. We each had lunch; she ate the school lunch, and I had brought my own sandwich. I also brought her most favorite snacks – fat free pretzels and an apple. At one point she jumped up en-thusiastically, did a little dance, and said, "Do you want to know what my Top Ten things in the world are?" I said, "Of course!" And here's what she said:

Number 10: Justin Bieber, Number 9: Justin Bieber, Number 8: Justin Bieber…and so on.

So, I guess like millions of other 10-year-old girls in this country, Nakiyah loves Justin Bieber. But it's the *enthusiasm* that I love about *her!* We talked and talked some more, and then she dramatically reached into her book bag and pulled out an envelope and handed it to me. Nanny had signed the permission slip! We will be visiting each other this summer!*

I know we're going to have some good times together, and I hope that Nakiyah benefits as much from this experience as I have. She's quite a girl.

.. .. ..

*Since I wrote this article, I've had two "summer dates" with Nakiyah. Here's a little taste of what went down:

1) She met my husband, Larry, for the first time, and over hot dogs and fries she looked at him appraisingly and said, "You know, Larry… there's something about you that I'm liking!" (Phew!)

2) She apologized to me about the "lizard neck" thing; I accepted her apology. (But I think I might still have a lizard neck!)

3) Justin Bieber is no longer #1; it's now Sandra Bullock!

4) Nakiyah informed me that she is planning to go to Harvard Law School to become a lawyer! (Look out Supreme Court!)

You GO girl…

I'M REALLY RICH! - (2013)

According to Webster's Dictionary, the word "rich" means "owning much money or property; having abundant possessions; wealthy". Now over the years, I've had *lots* of money…not *so much* money…not *enough* money…you get the picture. At this point in my life I don't have to worry about money, so I feel very lucky about that.

"Rich" is also defined as "well endowed; magnificently impressive". OK… in all honesty I must say that in my life men have found me attractive (at least my husband says *he* does), but…I am certainly NOT well endowed! Hey…that's a RICH one! (a sarcastic phrase meaning whatever was just said has amused you!)

"Rich" in experience implies "having more than enough to gratify normal needs or desires", and I've been fortunate enough to have had wonderful parents…a fantastic husband…terrific children and grandchildren. And the fact that I'm a writer – with hundreds of songs and articles to my credit – is as gratifying as it gets!

Now I want to talk about a very specific part of my life which has become quite important to me. If you've read my piece about Nakiyah, then you know that a little over ten years ago I decided that I would like to volunteer as a mentor to children who might need a bit of help. Finally, after all the girls had gone on to the middle school, at the beginning of this school year I met sisters Natasha (Fifth Grade) and Anjelica (Third Grade), and although the after-school programs had been cut due to the economy, my special relationship with the social worker enabled me to meet with them one day a week in the school library during their lunch period. It was truly magical. After some time – and after getting explicit permission from their parents – we also got together after school. I would pick them up at their home during a weekend or a school holiday, and we would go to a museum…or we'd go swimming in my community pool…and sometimes my husband and I would take them to a great Japanese Hibachi restaurant for dinner. They loved it!

This year Natasha is in the middle school, so it was just Anjelica and me. A few months ago Anjelica suggested that her friend Jancy join us in our Thursday lunch sessions, and after more permission slips, she did. I bring them little apple juice boxes, pears or apples (we love comparing Green, Macintosh, Delicious, Granny Smith, etc.), and (my old stand-by) fat-free pretzels. I was out-of-town on vacation the week of Valentine's Day, but when I arrived the next week, they presented me with a big shopping bag. I said, "What's this?" And they said with smiles, "It's a *Valentimes* gift for you!" I looked in the bag and saw an adorable mini-stuffed animal holding a big red heart which had the words "I love you" written on it. They both said, "We missed you on *Valentimes* Day…and you always bring us stuff…so we wanted to give something to you!" They had each written me a little note telling me how much they "love me and *upreceated* (appreciated) me". (I think we'll work on spelling next time!)

I was touched beyond words. How very sweet they were! What a happy "*Valentimes* Day"…and after removing the two letters they had written to me…I noticed that a single dollar bill was in the shopping bag. I immediately said, "Girls…I think maybe someone dropped this in the bag by accident…and I held out the dollar to them. They both said, "No…that's part of your gift from us!!"

So…that's why…I'M REALLY RICH!!!!

5
Travel Stories

Niagara Falls

London

Paris

Why I Like Budget-Rent-A-Car - (2008)

No...this is *not* an advertisement! Think of it more as an adventure. A *happy* adventure. Let me explain.

It all started on one of our many trips to our place in sunny Florida. There we were on our Jet Blue flight – midway – when I suddenly realized that I had forgotten to bring my sunglasses. *Darn!* I told Larry how annoyed at myself I was, and he calmly and reasonably said that we'd pick up an inexpensive pair for the week. So that settled that.

A couple of hours – and a safe landing (*thank-goodness-cause-I-hate-to-fly)* later, we were strolling through the Palm Beach Airport. Each time we travel we rent a car from whichever company gives us the best rate. This particular time it was Budget. We approached the counter, did the paperwork, and walked outside to wait for the Budget airport bus, which would deliver us to our Mercury compact.

Five minutes later we stopped at a lovely silver car, which was still dripping from having been thoroughly washed. It looked really shiny and clean. We put our suitcases in the trunk and got into the car. It was a very new car, and so we were checking out all the gadgets and gizmos before we inserted the key in the ignition. "Here's the air conditioner; here's the AM/FM/XM radio; here's the windshield wipers; and...oh look...here's where we would keep my sunglasses if I had remembered them!" I pressed a button right by the rear view mirror... and a little compartment opened up...and out popped a pair of Dolce & Gabbana sunglasses! DOLCE & GABBANA!!! Like on "Sex and the City"!!! They were absolutely gorgeous! Much nicer than the ones I left at home!! We must have laughed all the way to our place!

When we arrived at our house, I quickly washed the glasses. (You never know where they've been!) They fit perfectly! A bit later I went on the computer and checked out the style number and discovered that these glasses sold for more than $150!

So you see...*THAT'S* why I *really* like Budget Rent-A-Car! All the latest in automobiles...and Dolce & Gabbana too!

Note: Yes, I *did* call Budget to see if anyone was missing anything...but no one was...so they're *mine! All mine!* End of story!

All A-Bored! - (2009)

I recently went to Baltimore to attend a family funeral. I decided to take the Amtrak – as opposed to flying (which I HATE to do, but *do* it anyway...but that's another story) – and so I started the first leg of my 4-hour "train journey" on the Long Island Railroad. I brought a book so I wouldn't be *bored*...but I forgot my reading glasses and couldn't see a word! (You might say I started off on the *wrong track!*)

When I was a little girl, we would make occasional train trips to Baltimore for various family occasions. My Dad would reserve a 'compartment' on the train, and so we would have our own little private traveling room. We always ate dinner in the Dining Car. What a fabulous experience that was! The waiters would take our orders, and there we were...on that speeding train...eating such delicacies as Welsh Rarebit, Hungarian Goulash, and other great treats. Those Baltimore trips were always exciting for me.

This time, when I arrived at Penn Station in New York, I had no idea where the Amtrak trains were; it had been a long time since I was there. I had purchased my round-trip tickets online, but unlike air travel, you can't print out your tickets at home; you have to either go to a ticket window or a kiosk at the station. There were about 400 people on line at the ticket window, and so I found myself at a kiosk desperately trying to figure out how to operate it. After about 5 tries, I did it! I had my tickets! Then all I had to do was wait for an announcement as to which track my train was on. The tension was mounting and as soon as track 18 East was announced, a stampede had formed. I followed the crowd and soon found that there are very few (if any) escalators going down to the trains. And my suitcase was really heavy! So I ruptured my arm and went down the stairs with the crowd. I watched out for the "gap between the train and the station"…and I somehow found an empty seat by a window. There was no way I could ever have lifted my suitcase to the rack above, and so I saw a strong-looking young man and asked for his help, which he gave me. I was hoping *he* was going to Baltimore. If not, I'd just have to leave my suitcase there!

One thing that was quite different from my childhood excursions was the fact that *everyone*, in *every* seat, had at least one cell phone, Blackberry, or laptop. The woman sitting next to me was working her Blackberry and answering two different cell phones, which she kept searching for in her pocketbook. It was a cacophony of doorbell chimes, rap music, and buzzing all around me. There were two men in the seat behind me conducting major financial transactions. I almost invested myself! (My luck…it would've been Bernie Madoff!)

And then…while stopped at the Wilmington station, we heard over the loudspeaker that there would be a delay because one of the passengers had been injured. I turned and saw that the injured person was actually in the back of the car I was in. Actually, she wasn't *injured* per se…it seems that – how should I put it – she was a bit overweight and couldn't seem to get out of her seat! The conductors were there; the police came, and finally, with a lot of hard work, she was thankfully extricated.

We arrived in Baltimore 15 minutes late…but I didn't have to deal with my 'fear of flying'…I didn't have to take off my shoes (although that would've come in handy if I had wanted to throw them at a world leader or something!)…and, no…it certainly wasn't *boring!*

"Double Duty" Vacation - (2012)

The Online Dictionary definition of the expression "Double Duty" is as follows: …to serve two purposes or have two functions…as in "She doubles as his wife and secretary." MY definition is quite different, and although I know that my Mom would have frowned at any kind of "bathroom humor", Double Duty will always mean something else to me! (You know what I'm talkin' about…right?)

For as long as I can remember, I've had IBS, Irritable Bowel Syndrome, which – in my case – means that I'm familiar with most of the rest-rooms in town! Actually, I'm used to it. Unfortunately, my handsome husband, Larry, was diagnosed with Colitis – after a sigmoidoscopy – on the day before we had a trip planned to Niagara Falls and Toronto. His doctor gave him medication and told us NOT to cancel our vaca-tion…and so we didn't cancel. I guess you could say that we both had "Traveler's Diarrhea" before we even started to travel!

The car service picked us up at our Long Island home the next morn-ing and delivered us to Delta's Terminal 3 at JFK on time for our flight to Buffalo, NY. We only had carry-on luggage, and so as we started to walk into the terminal, we noticed a sign saying that the terminal for our flight had been changed to Terminal 2. Now at JFK Airport, Terminal 2 is in NO WAY walking distance from Terminal 3! At that moment, we saw our driver driving away…but somehow, waving fran-tically, we caught his attention, and he picked us up again and drove us to the correct place. Whew!

Now we were at Terminal 2 and found that we had at least an hour be-fore our flight was boarding. We noticed a cute little café and decided to have brunch. We each had a croissant and egg sandwich and iced tea. It was good! But when my husband got the check…it WASN'T good! The check was for $71.75! I mean…*really!* We all know that air-port food is expensive, but this was ridiculous! So of course Larry took the check to the cashier and pointed out this error. She agreed it was an error, but didn't know how to correct it in their computer. She made a phone call to her manager, who was in another part of the airport. And so we waited for the manager. Finally, he was able to correct the mistake, and our brunch bill was a measly $31.00! And since it took so much time, we walked out of there only to see huge lines of passengers boarding at our gate. We got on the end of the line, and only as we approached the gate did we realize that this flight was heading for Los Angeles…not Buffalo. Oops! Our gate was the next one over! And now *they* were boarding too! We made it onto the plane, and the flight was smooth and uneventful. Except for the fact that the young guy in the seat in front of Larry was leaning so far back that my husband's knees were black and blue! When I leaned over in an attempt to ask this kid to adjust his seat, I saw that this young man was busily…uh…let's say "cleaning out his nose"! And so I chose not to converse with him! (My Mom wouldn't have liked me to discuss this either!) My husband's knees would just have to suffer!

We had a smooth flight (thank goodness cause I'm a nervous flier) and went directly to Avis where we had a compact car reserved. Since Larry is an Avis honors member, all we had to do was go downstairs where all the cars were and find out where ours was parked. The pleasant lady at the booth took our name and told us that our car was in spot J-13. Well, when we got to J-13, it certainly wasn't a compact car. It was a humongous RV! Way too big for our needs! We would have needed a ladder just to get into it! So we went back to the lady and told her that it must be a mistake since we had ordered a compact car. She looked quite confused, and then walked us back to the car. "Yes", she said. "That is definitely *not* your car. Your car is in J-11." And yes…there was our cute little compact. "Sorry", she said. *"Our Bad!"*

We followed our Mapquest directions to our hotel. No problem there. It took us about a half hour. Our hotel was across the street from the Casino and right near the Falls, and the whole area was absolutely buzzing with people! Tourists from everywhere! We pulled into the driveway of the hotel parking lot, and the attendant asked if we wanted valet parking or self-parking. Although valet parking was $10 extra per day, Larry said "Valet, please". So we drove up a bit further, as instructed, but...no one was there. And so we parked in the first available space we saw. Nobody gave us a ticket, so we proceeded to the lobby to check in.

During the days we walked down the hill to see the Falls up close. What a beautiful sight. We opted NOT to go on the boat which actually travels *under* the Falls. (You really don't want to be under Niagara Falls on a boat and looking for the restroom!) We also went to an IMAX theatre which told all about the history of the area...and it was fascinating! We checked out the Casino for a short time each day, and, once we understood the exchange rate of US dollars to Canadian dollars, we had fun!

The first night we went to a fabulous Brazilian Restaurant. They come around to your table every few minutes with another unbelievable steak...chicken...shrimp...whatever concoction and add it to your plate. Because of his colitis pain, Larry wasn't eating anything! All these luscious dishes...and NADA! I had no idea at the time exactly how very much he was suffering, but I have to admit...*I* thought the food was amazing! The second night he felt a bit better, and we dined at the restaurant on the top floor of our hotel with a total view of Niagara Falls. It was heavenly!

We didn't use our car again until we were setting out for Toronto. As we went through the exit, we expected someone to tell us how much we owed for parking there, but the attendant seemed to be in a hurry, and he impatiently waved us on...and out the exit! Wow! That was almost as exciting as winning four sixes at the slot machine at the Casino. (Too bad we had only bet fifty cents on that one!)

Two hours later we arrived in Toronto, and boy is that a beautiful city!

Our hotel was lovely. No problems there. Larry's old friend, whom I had never met before and who has been living in Toronto for years, picked us up and drove us to his home. His wife was lovely as was his young daughter. After drinks and hors d'oeuvres we all went to a very nice nearby restaurant. The food was delicious, but, unfortunately our friend's wife and daughter never got served their dinner! The waiter was quite apologetic, but the good news was…no bill! This was starting to be a "regular thing" with us! (No charge for parking; no charge for dinner!) The next day we toured the city. The Yorkville area was spectacular where we had wonderful reflexology foot treatments on the spur of the moment…and then we had a terrific dinner at a restaurant near our hotel.

We had been warned that it might take quite a bit of time at the border driving back to the Buffalo airport. Our returning flight was at 2:30 in the afternoon, but we left the hotel at 9:00 AM. It's a good thing! As we approached the bridge that connects the US and Canada, all the traffic slowed down. Two hours later we reached the border, they checked our passports, and we continued the drive to the Buffalo airport. Happily, we made it on time for our flight, which, once again, was smooth. Our taxi was waiting, and we got home safely.

All in all we had a wonderful time…but I'm sure you can now see what I was talking about. And…there was absolutely *nothing* that was duty-free!

I'M A LOSER! - (2013)

Well…not really. Well…maybe! Let me explain. I'm a senior citizen, and ever since that happened to me ("Senior Citizenship"), I seem to *lose* things: like my concentration when I'm telling an involved story; like my composure when I laugh at something I'm not supposed to laugh at; and like my reading glasses. Here's a little story to prove my point.

My husband Larry and I took a short vacation to Delray Beach, Florida (a lovely town) not so long ago. (Don't ask me for dates… 'cause I forget.) The flight was fine – although a little too bumpy for me…*just saying* – and we landed at the West Palm Beach airport. I had MapQuested the directions from the airport to the hotel, and since I had no problem reading those directions, I KNOW I had my reading glasses then. We decided to have dinner at our hotel that night, and since I was able to read the menu, I KNOW I had my reading glasses then! However, the next morning, I couldn't find my reading glasses…*anywhere!*

At home, I have maybe a half dozen pairs of reading glasses…in the kitchen (for recipes), in my office (for business), in the living room (books and newspapers), in the bedroom (for the crossword late at night…don't ask), and in basically all the other rooms in our house. (I really hate them in my bathroom when I'm putting on my makeup and I can see every damn line in my face! I'd rather not see so clearly!). Anyway…I'm never at a loss for reading glasses!

But now, on this vacation…here's what happened. That first morning we went to the front desk at our hotel and asked the young lady there if a pair of glasses had been found. After she checked and told us "no", I *knew* I had lost my reading glasses…and I knew that I *needed new ones* in order to have a decent time on this trip. So when Larry and I went out to lunch on beautiful Atlantic Avenue, I couldn't read the menu, so he read it for me. We had a delightful lunch, but when we finished, and he had several business calls to make, I decided to go across the street to a drugstore and buy a new pair of reading glasses. Fortunately, they had a nice selection, and I found a pair that was just fine. I paid for them and went back to the outdoor area where I had left my husband. He had finished his business calls, and, as we were walking back to our lovely hotel, I realized that I no longer had my *sun* glasses – which I thought had been on top of my head. OK. So, while I was buying a new pair of reading glasses…I LOST MY SUNGLASSES!!! Could that possibly be?? Yes…it could!

This was getting weirder and weirder. There was a store on the way back to our hotel which sold sun glasses, and Larry insisted upon buying me a pair. I think he wanted to calm me down! Anyway, when we got back, we stopped by the front desk – again – and I asked if a pair of sunglasses had been found. The young lady kind of looked at me suspiciously. Wasn't I the same woman who had asked earlier about a missing pair of reading glasses? Was this some sort of "Glasses Scam"? Well, she slowly picked up a pair of sunglasses holding them close to her chest. "Are these yours?" *YES!! They were my missing sunglasses! Thank you very much!* And as we headed toward the elevators, I saw her looking at us and shaking her head. So now I had two pairs of sun glasses since I couldn't return the new ones having removed all the stickers from them only moments ago.

Talking about losing things, the very next day Larry couldn't find his cell phone. Now *this* was serious! We looked everywhere in our room, but he was thinking he had left it at the restaurant we had been at the night before. This restaurant was a forty-five minute car ride from our hotel, but he was ready to drive there at ten in the morning. "Glasses – Smasses!" but a cell phone is business…it's life…it's survival! Happily, upon getting into our rented car, Larry found his phone, and so he didn't have to make the drive. Phew!

I managed to retain all 3 pairs of my glasses for the remainder of our trip. Larry still has his phone. And except for the tornado warnings on our last night – this vacation was a *winner!*

"Weak" in London and Paris! - (2013)

Weak with joy and excitement, that is! My husband, Larry, and I just returned from an amazing week in London and Paris. *Blimey!* It was *magnifique!* But it certainly started out on the wrong foot!

We had signed up with the wonderful Tauck tour group, and they suggested that we get to the airport (JFK) three hours prior to our flight to London. The flight was at 9:15 PM, and so we asked the car service to pick us up at 5:30 since rush-hour traffic in Long Island – where we live – is pretty hectic. The car service had been recommended by our new next-door neighbor who had told us Bobby, the driver, was really good. We were all packed and ready to go… passports safely in place, and 5:30 ticked by…then 5:45…and so on. We tried calling him several times, but only got a busy signal. I called our neighbor and asked if Bobby might have another number, but he didn't. The next minute our neighbor was at our door waiting to take us to JFK! What a generous thing to do…especially since he and his wife were expecting company for dinner! But we accepted because we really needed to get to that airport quickly! The good news about this episode is that when we were only about 10 minutes from home, Bobby called Larry's cell, told us that he had thought the pick-up time was 6:00, and that he was on his way to meet us at a nearby gas station and drive us the rest of the way to the airport. Whew! That worked out just fine…and our neighbor got home to his wife and his dinner guests!

We got to JFK in plenty of time; checked in; did all the stuff you're supposed to do, and had time to sit down at an airport restaurant. We each ordered a drink and a sandwich, and the bill only came to $100! (Hey, that's airport restaurants for you! What can ya do!) We boarded our flight to London on time, and 7 hours and 20 minutes later, we arrived! Many passengers on the flight were sleeping; not me. I can barely sleep in my bed, but that's another story! So it's around 4:00 AM in my head, but it's actually now 9:00 AM in London. We were picked up by a driver sent by our tour and arrived at our gorgeous hotel, The Churchill, in about an hour. Our room was lovely!

The welcome cocktail reception/dinner at our hotel was fun. We got to meet all the other people on our tour. The food was delicious; the drinks wonderful (I've never been known to dislike a drink...but that's another story!). And the people...what a terrific variety of men and women from all over the USA. Over the course of the week, we got to know several of them quite well. Just to point out a few, there were Linda and Ron from California (friendly, funny, perky); Pete and Maria from New Jersey (also friendly and kind; sorry Maria that I kept calling you Wendy! Don't exactly know why; maybe it was the time change...or maybe the drink!); Sandy from Florida (sweet and gushing with personality); Jeanine from Arizona (a bit handicapped in the 'walking department', but not one bit handicapped in enthusiasm!); the "young couple", Adib and Elizabeth from Texas (smart and romantic); the 4 couples we called "The Reading Group" from Reading, PA (which happens to be where I was born, but since I moved from there at age 2 ½ , I didn't remember any of them!); the 2 lovely ladies from Connecticut, Barbara and Carol (nobody mixed us up cause my name has an "e" at the end!); Patti and Dargin from California (you can't forget *his* name!); and others from Manhattan, Virginia, Tennessee, Illinois, and Maryland. Our adorable young tour guide, Charlie (short for Charlotte) is from Massachusetts. So now you get the picture of the variety of personalities we were among. A very special group!

The next day in London we visited Windsor Castle, built in the 11th century, and the longest occupied palace in Europe. Later, on to Westminster Abbey, architecturally exquisite, it is not only the burial place of certain royalty, but it was there that Prince William married Kate Middleton. Kind of mind-blowing to say the least! On Day 3 we saw the Tower of London which holds the Crown Jewels (you really need to have a huge head if you're going to be royalty in England!), and that evening we went to the theatre district and saw "Mathilda", one of the best musicals ever! Day 4 was the British Museum (it certainly had NOT lost its charm!)…but even better than that was afternoon tea at Fortnum & Mason, the legendary department store. (Just for the record, scones with clotted cream had been recommended to me by a friend before I left on this journey, and from now on I will do *whatever* she recommends!)

The next day we took the Eurostar train through the "Chunnel" to Paris. Upon arriving our bus took us to Le Grand Hotel, another beauty! Day 6 took us to Versailles filled with so much historical and beautiful artwork…and of course fabulous gardens as well. Later our bus took us to Montmartre, a city of artists and poets. All this time I had been hoping that the French I had taken in school would serve me well, and it did…as long as people spoke VERY, VERY slowly! Day 7 was when we came face to face with Mona Lisa at the Louvre. Wow! (But I was amazed at how small that painting is compared to all the others.) And the day was capped off with a farewell dinner cruise on which we all said adieu to Paris.

The next morning Larry and I were picked up at our hotel at 9:40 AM. Our flight was at 1:40 PM, but it's all about customs and immigration…that kind of stuff. The flight was smooth, the flight attendants helpful, and we arrived back at JFK at around 4:00 PM New York time. For us it was 10:00 PM. Then we went through customs and immigration. That took about an hour. We got our luggage and called Bobby (this time he was right on time!) and got back home at 6:00 (midnight for us), went to a local place for pizza (we were hungry), and went to bed local time at 8…but 2:00 AM for us!

The tiredness has mostly worn off, but the happy and exciting memories of London, Paris, and all those wonderful, friendly people will NEVER wear off.

6

Love Stories

Our Wedding! February 13, 2010

"…TOO OLD…TO REALLY BE IN LOVE"? - (2012)

Remember the hit song "Too Young" by Nat King Cole? *"They try to tell us we're too young. Too young to really be in love…"* Well, I'm here today to prove that you're never *too old* to be in love!

I got married at the age of 24, and of course I thought it would last forever. But more than a quarter of a century later, that marriage would come to an end. We had many good times; we had two wonderful children; we had several successful businesses over the years; but we also had problems that we just couldn't overcome. Along with emotional scars came financial issues and business problems. Without going into detail, I'll just say that at a certain point we both realized it wasn't working any more. And so we separated, and within a year or two, we got divorced. I'm glad to say that we have maintained a friendly relationship with each other to this day.

So there I was…a woman over 50… *"OUT there"*! Since our house was sold in anticipation of our divorce, I had moved to a much smaller home. It was located a block away from the beach on the South shore of Long Island and a few blocks away from the tennis club of which I was a member for many years. I have always loved tennis, and playing in a great tennis game was extremely helpful to me during this very difficult time. I had a lot of friends there – women *and* men – who were very supportive, and we always had fun. There were also people who played there whom I *didn't* know and *wasn't* friendly with…and Larry was one of them!

I *did* know – by judging from the men he played tennis with – that he was a bit older than I, and I had heard that he was separated as well. I *also* knew – just by looking at him – that he was a very handsome man! At some point during that summer, while a big crowd was watching a club championship tournament on center court, Larry started a conversation with me. He was extremely charming and funny, and when he invited me to join him for a lunch date, I didn't hesitate. We had a wonderful meal and great conversation…and when the subject of "age" came up, he told me that he was seven years my senior. No problem with *that!*

We kept seeing each other and the relationship got quite serious. We truly made each other very happy. It wasn't until I was *in love* with him that I found out that he had lied to me about his age. He was really 14 years older than me! Oh well…*love conquers all!* (And I believe that was the *only* lie he ever told me…and I'm glad he *did!*) Both of our divorces came through, and after some time we decided to "move in" together. We also decided we'd move to the North shore of Long Island and start our new life together in a new locale. He found a lovely home in 1998, and I moved in with him six months later. We made new friends while keeping the old, and we played lots of tennis at our new condominium community.

In January, 2010, after eleven happy years living together, we were spending a Friday afternoon out and about. Some sad things had happened recently to some close friends and family, and we were just talking about that. We looked at each other and almost at the exact same time, we said, "What could we do that would be a *happy* thing for a change?" And we both answered: *"Let's get married!"* And so, a month and a half later, after we worked out the plans with our adult children, Larry and I got married at our favorite restaurant. One of our close friends, who is a judge, married us in front of our families and good friends.

We'll be celebrating our third anniversary this February. It's working out great! And every day we tell each other how madly in love we are. I'm going to be 70 at my next birthday, and he'll soon be 84.

So, Nat King Cole *sort* of had it right when he sang that song, but I've changed the words just a bit…

> "…And yet we're not too *old* to know
> This love will last though years may go
> And then some day they may recall
> We were not too *old* at all…"

SHACKING UP WITH SANDY: The Only Funny Thing About The Hurricane - (2012)

Well, not exactly shacking up! Let me explain. I live in Jericho on the North Shore of Long Island, New York, and when Hurricane Sandy came barreling through, it was pretty scary. That storm was fierce and unforgiving, and it caused a great deal of hardship and tragic loss for many Long Island residents. We were among the luckier ones, and we only lost power for 8 days. My husband, Larry, and I are Senior citizens, but we're both healthy, and we weren't worried about anything serious…health-wise (As long as one of the gigantic old trees didn't fall on our house and kill us!).

We have friends and family members who live within 45 minutes of our home – and who never lost their power – and so we stayed as guests at *their* homes for a few days. We had actually tried to get a room at several hotels closer to our house, but they were totally booked up. We felt lucky to have been invited to our friend's and family's homes, but it was quite a trek to travel there and then back to our house to get clothing and other necessities and to check everything out. None of the traffic lights were working, and it was kind of scary to drive through all the busy intersections. Also, the gas lines were unbelievable! I was especially glad that I had filled up my Hybrid car prior to the storm.

At some point an idea came to me: Five minutes from our lovely suburban neighborhood is a very commercial area with a Home Depot, Staples, Dunkin' Donuts, etc. And it occurred to me that there were a few "Day-Rate/Sleazy" Motels right in that area. I had never really noticed or thought of them before. Now remember, I'm in my late 60s, and Larry's a decade older. But we thought, "Wouldn't it be great to have TV and a hot shower…and be just around the corner from home?" So we drove into the parking area of the first DRS (day-rate-sleazy) Motel. The guy in the office looked at us peculiarly and said, "How can I help you?" Larry asked, "Do you have a room available?"

The guy glanced at me and then back at Larry. "How many hours?" said he. "Overnight" we both said at the same time. He shrugged and told us it would be $110 payment up front. Larry very cleverly then said, "Can we take a look at the room first?" and the guy said "Sure". We walked up some creepy outdoor steps and got to room 27. We opened the door and took a whiff and simultaneously shook our heads *NO*. Don't *think* so!! Too smelly for us! And so we disappointedly got back into our car.

We figured we'd give it one more try since there was another DRS motel across the street. We went through the same process...the same peculiar look...and then we took a look at the room they had to offer. Not bad! (Not great...but not bad at all!) So we paid the guy the money up front, and then we drove home to get supplies. By "supplies" I mean pillow cases and towels, and we threw some clothes into a bag and drove back to our nice warm room. What we hadn't noticed before while checking out the room was a detail on the four-poster king-sized bed. There was a huge mirror across the top! I must admit, it was rather interesting and different to be lying in bed, looking up, and seeing the two of us as if we were on a big screen TV! Gee...I hope there was no hidden camera!

Anyway, we stayed at the DRS #2 for a few days, and we even recommended it to friends who were also without power. They actually were in the room right next door, but we refrained from putting our ears to the wall! Finally, we heard that the lights were back on in our community, and although we had already paid for another night, we happily and speedily went home. Unfortunately, neighbors just up the street lost their power again, and so we told them to use our motel room...and they did. Hope they enjoyed!

Happily for us, we're all back in our homes now. There was damage, but not like what many people in the New York/New Jersey area faced. Just in case my story sounds far-fetched, check out the picture of Larry and me in our very sexy and sleazy motel mirrored bed! (Hey, everybody needs to catch up on their sleep sometimes!)

Shacking Up With Hurricane Sandy

7

Funny Stuff

Wonderful singer Deena Miller and me in a scene from my youtube
"Food Is Better Than Sex!"

My little grandson Walker LOVES funny stuff!

FOR A SONG… - (2007)

I *used* to be a songwriter. A lyricist, actually. I wrote the words, and various composers wrote the music. I started about 30 years ago when I discovered that I had a knack for rhyming. I attended a songwriters' workshop in Manhattan, and I *just knew* that I'd be the next Marvin Hamlisch. Well, OK…maybe Carole Bayer Sager. (At least we spell our names the same way!) When a collaborator and I completed a song, we would then produce a demo recording, which involved hiring a professional singer and back-up musicians and then recording the song onto an audio cassette.

I must have written hundreds of songs. There were disco songs (hey, it was the 80s!), ballads, novelty songs, show tunes, and country songs. And if I say so myself, most of them were really good! Five of my songs were actually published and recorded on various labels. One made it to the Billboard Country Music Charts. One made it to the Shari Lewis "Lambchop Show". But basically, it was so difficult to get someone to listen to a song written by an "unknown" that I decided to pursue other interests.

Now it's 30 years later, and I rediscovered about 50 audio cassettes in my garage. I dusted them off, searched the Internet, and found a company in Long Island that could transfer the songs onto CDs (hey, it's 2007!). I learned how to enter the songs onto my hard drive and then how to "burn" various songs onto blank CDs so I could start sending them out to artists, agents, and record labels. And now I remember that old feeling: *REJECTION!*

Although I've had a bit of interest so far, I've also encountered the following: "We only accept submissions from major labels" or "We do not accept unsolicited material". It's like someone applying for a job and is told that they only hire people with experience in that very job. How does one get experience if no one gives him the chance? You see what I mean?!! It's very frustrating. But I'm not going to give up this time.

After all, when you have a novelty show song entitled *"Food Is Better Than Sex"* with lyrics like *I love to sink my teeth into a lobster claw / And I love eating oysters - 'specially when they're in the raw! When I need to satisfy myself / All that I need – is my grocer's shelf!* And what about the country song *I'm gonna take you back to the store / Baby, you're no good anymore…* Or the song I wrote about a shopping bag lady, *Bag Lady, who'd you use to be / Did you have the hopes and dreams – of young girls like me…* or one of the last songs I wrote called *I'm As Blue as the Blue in your Eyes*, in honor of my guy, Larry. (You *must* have noticed his eyes!)

I absolutely *love* to write lyrics. The process, alone, makes me happy. So, even if I'm rejected (again), I'm having a fantastic time reconnecting with all my songs. And if *anybody* knows *anybody* - who knows *anybody* in the music business, please…send them my way! You never know…I could be a star!!

Coupon Carole - (2008)

I think it all started for me when I learned how to write emails. In the "old" days, if I were dissatisfied with a product, I would never write a letter to the company and complain. That was never my style. But now…all I have to do is Google the brand name and go onto their web site. Easy! I can think of four examples…right off the top of my head!

(1) A couple of years ago, while in Florida, we went to a Red Lobster Restaurant. I was in one of my hungry lobster-and-nothing-else-could-satisfy-me moods. The waitress approached our table, and I ordered a steamed lobster…female (I *know* my lobsters). And that's when she said, "Sorry, we're all out of lobsters!" Well, the next day as I was getting over my depression from the lobster-less night before, I found the Red Lobster web site on my computer, and I wrote

a friendly letter of complaint. "How could Red Lobster be out of lobsters?" I asked. And I felt immediately better having written to them. I wasn't expecting any kind of answer. Truthfully! About a week later I received a letter of apology and a $15 coupon to Red Lobster!

(2) I hate to admit it, but I've been kind of hooked on a Hammacher/Schlemmer gizmo called a sleep/sound machine. It all started over 25 years ago when there was noisy construction right near my home on the south shore of Long Island. The machine emits a white noise, which blocks out all other noises, and it was the only thing that allowed me to sleep. Recently, it just died. The silence was unbearable. I decided to write to Hammacher/Schlemmer to find out what might have caused this. I got an immediate reply saying that this item comes with a lifetime guarantee, and if I sent my defective one back to them (plus $5 since the price had gone up), they would send me a brand new one. I did…and they did! (The current price, by the way, is over $53!)

(3) I make a great tuna fish salad hors d'oeuvre! I'm known for it. And so recently I opened a can of Bumble Bee (Solid White in Water), got out the rest of my secret ingredients, and I started to prepare my famous dish. I noticed that the tuna had a yellowish tint as opposed to the usual pink color. Nevertheless, I mashed, and I mixed, and I thought I had just better taste it to make sure. It was awful! It was so sour I dumped the whole thing. As you might guess, later that day I wrote an email to Bumble Bee. I told them where I bought it, and I even gave them the 9 or 10 digit number which was printed on the can. One week later I received a letter of apology and coupons for 2 cans of Bumble Bee (Solid White in Water).

(4) And finally…last Monday, after my weekly supermarket shopping, I decided to prepare one of my favorite chicken dishes. It involves light soy sauce, minced garlic, pepper, parsley, and other spices. I

marinate the chicken pieces in this blend and broil it. It's really delicious. I had purchased a package of Perdue Whole Chicken Cut-Up Parts. I opened the package in my sink and washed each piece separately. I couldn't believe it, but I soon realized there was only one drumstick in the package. I even checked inside my sink's garbage disposal…but yes…there was only one leg! Did I get a handicapped chicken? Hmmm. Well, I cooked the rest of it, and we enjoyed it immensely. But…yes…you guessed it, I wrote to Perdue. I asked – in a rather humorous email – if it was possible that I had gotten a chicken with only one leg! Yesterday I received a phone call from Perdue. The woman assured me that all their chickens have two legs…and that my email had made her day! She said that the parts are packed by hand, and she also told me to be expecting a $3 coupon in the mail this week! I told her that it really wasn't necessary, but she insisted. Oh well.

So that's all I can report so far, but just think what would happen if (only) something went wrong with the pen I got as a gift from Tiffany's; you know…I really love diamonds…

Funny Words - (2009)

As I was whizzing through the aisles of the supermarket today, filling my cart with all the essentials I would need for the week, I was very intent on hurrying through because I had a business appointment, and I didn't want to be late. I was trying to steer my wayward cart through the myriad of shoppers, some of whom were clogging the aisles as they were reading the ingredients on a box of I Can't Believe It's Not Butter, or others who were scrutinizing a can of Chicken With Stars Soup. (Each a fascinating read!) Really, though…they should have little traffic signs to ease all the congestion…or at *least* one-way aisles. Anyway, while in the *salad dressing and condiment* aisle, I overheard a bit of conversation, which actually made me stop and chuckle out loud. An elderly couple was "cart-browsing", unfortunately tying up all the other cart traffic. I was really not paying any attention to them until the moment the woman said to the man (whom I assume was her husband) in a very loud New York accent much like George's mother on "Seinfeld", *"How're ya doin' with your pickles?"* For whatever reason, this completely cracked me up! I finished my shopping with a smile on my face.

Here's another story – completely unrelated to that one – but it also illustrates how certain words can make you laugh. Many, many years ago, when I was a young bride, my (ex)husband and I moved into a New York City apartment in the West 70s. It was the first floor of a brownstone - small, but nice. We hired a painter to paint the living room, which really needed it. He was a nice guy with a really thick German accent. On the first day he told me that he would need me to get more *"schpahkel"* – or at least that's what it sounded like to me! After all, how would a young girl who grew up in Long Island know what *spackle* is anyway? Or that it rhymes with "tackle"? So I went to the hardware store and asked the guy for *"schpahkel"*…and of course he looked at me like I was an idiot. Needless to say, I left that store without the spackle.

To this day I still think of it as *"schpahkel"*, and there's nothing that could make me think of it in any other way! It seems that once a word is embedded in your mind, it kind of stays there like that. So…if I should ever notice a crack in our wall here in our lovely New York home, I will be sending my guy out to the store to get the *"schp----"*, well, you know what I mean!

FLOSSING AGAIN… - (2012)

No, this is *not* a dental article. I'll explain that in a minute. This is about how quickly the time is passing. The older I get, the more quickly it passes…and that's just the way it is. About twenty years ago I had periodontal surgery. My upper right quadrant (don't know if that's the technical term, but I'm sure you know what I mean) was inflamed, and my 'regular' dentist sent me to the periodontist. He said that I needed the surgery to basically save my teeth. And so *of course* I had the surgery. *Man…that hurt!* He told me that if I flossed diligently every day that I could most probably avoid further surgery….and more importantly to *me*…have a pretty smile. But he wasn't just talking about a "quick floss" – the quick in-and-out between each tooth; no, he was talking about 20 to 25 seconds between teeth…and carefully concentrating on the edges of each tooth. "Sure", I said, "I can do that! No problem!"

I've been doing that for twenty years now. Every night, before I turn out the light, I floss. If I happen to fall asleep *without* flossing, I suddenly wake up at three in the morning, and…yes…I floss! But here's the thing: I'm ALWAYS flossing! Each day starts differently. Some days I do a lot of chores. I make the bed; I do the laundry; I go to the supermarket; I clean the house. Some days I have appointments. I go to the doctor (general…gynecologist…neurologist…depending on what's hurting and what's not hurting). Some days I create. I write songs; I write articles (like this one); I write poems for parties. Some days I spend with children. I have lunch with my married son and/or married daughter and/or their spouses; I visit/babysit my three little grandsons; I mentor two adorable sisters at a local elementary school. Some days I play. I'm an avid tennis player, and I absolutely love it (though I used to be better when I was younger, but then again, *everything's* better when you're younger!).

Speaking of waking up in the middle of the night…even on nights when I *did* remember to floss, I often have awakened several times during the night anyway. I'd wake up at 1:30, and then again at 4:00… and then I had a night when I didn't sleep at all. How I longed for the good old days of only waking up twice! I've had (non)sleeping issues for years, and I've always dealt with them. But recently, at one of my doctor-appointment days (see above), I was advised to take a "sleep test" at home. This involved a gentleman coming to my house and instructing me on this piece of equipment I was to wear while I slept that night. It would record my breathing, my non-breathing, and lots of other pertinent information about my sleep habits. I think these instructions were comparable to those given at NASA headquarters. I had to wrap this Velcro item around my left arm, put my ring finger through a sticky Band-aid type thing, put my pointer through a tubular device, and attach 2 sticky do-hickys to my throat and chest. And then just go to sleep…right? Yeah, right!

Well, I did actually fall asleep, and the machine actually monitored whatever it was supposed to. On my follow-up visit to that doctor, he told me that I had a mild form of Apnea and that I should go to a special dentist who makes mouth devices for people with problems such as mine. He also told me to get a "side" pillow - which would help me to sleep on my side - which is apparently better than sleeping on my back - which might be the reason I keep waking up. I got the pillow, and all it did for me was decrease my bank account by ninety-five dollars! I seem to be managing my life pretty well even without a good 8 hours each night. I recently got re-married to a wonderful man; my kids are happy; my life is good. Still, at the end of every day, what happens? I'M FLOSSING!

Well, at least my teeth are clean!

LOBSTER TALES 2 - (2013)

Those who have read my book* (all five of you) might recall the piece I wrote called "Lobster Tales". It told the story of the time my husband and I were in Florida, and we decided to go to the local Red Lobster Restaurant. I absolutely LOVE lobster. I love it steamed with butter sauce on the side, and I love sucking out all that delicious meet from the little legs...the claws...*whatever!* Anyway, when the waitress came to our table, I happily gave her my order, and – hard to believe – but she told us that they were OUT of lobsters! Red Lobster OUT of lobsters??? How could that possibly be? Well, the good news is that after I wrote them a letter, they sent me a coupon, and...I wrote a pretty cute article about it, and so it wasn't a *total* tragedy!

As they say in the movie business, cut to a few years later. Last week, as I was doing my regular weekly supermarket shopping, I saw that the Sea Food Department was having a sale on fresh lobsters! Instead of the usual $9.99 per pound, it was $5.99 per pound, and so I headed over to that part of the store. There were two "Sea Food guys" (I don't know what else to call them!) behind the counter, and the younger one said, "Can I help you?" I said the following: "I'd like 2 small lobsters, but... please...I want you to make sure they're dead!" I stipulate this whenever I order lobsters after having seen the movie "Annie Hall" years ago. There was an unforgettable scene in which Woody Allen's and Diane Keaton's characters try to cook live lobsters, and in the process of dropping them in the boiling water, the lobsters screamed and wiggled... and well, you just wouldn't EVER want to experience THAT!

So the Sea Food guy went in the back room and shortly came back with a large see-through plastic bag containing the lobsters. He put them on the counter, and...THEY WERE CRAWLING ALL OVER EACH OTHER! Every little leg was moving and scratching! I said, "I wanted them DEAD!" He replied, I killed them. The older guy was observing all this, and he spoke to his co-worker: "They're NOT dead! You gotta split them with your knife!" The younger guy rolled his eyes while shaking his head. He grabbed the bag and said, "OK...OK...I'll kill them *again!*" I'm starting to feel a little guilty at this point, but not enough to take wiggling, scriggling lobsters home!

Finally, the lobsters were delivered to me the way I had requested. I steamed mine, broiled my husband's with breadcrumbs on top, and we really enjoyed our dinner.

This week I was shopping at the same Supermarket. I was in a hurry and rather pre-occupied while wheeling my cart in and out of the aisles. Suddenly there was a huge commotion! Some crazy guy was running through the aisles, pushing carts aside, and screaming obscenities. I was really scared, and when I heard him getting closer to me, I quickly moved my cart to the side of the soup aisle. He saw me do that, and he made a punching motion with his arm…knocked down about 20 Cream of Mushroom soups…and started talking to ME: "You made me a murderer! You made me KILL those poor lobsters!" It was the young Sea Food Guy! He was coming closer and closer…and then…I woke up! It was just a bad dream! Phew!

Now, every time I think about the whole experience, I have a good laugh. Hope *you* do too! (Hope lobsters don't go on sale too soon again!)

FUNNY IS FUNNY! - (2013)

So I'm at the car wash waiting for my car, and there are a few people standing and sitting around. An older woman - who obviously works for the car wash place – was trimming the carnations in the window boxes which surround the entire glassed-in room. It's a small room, so we're all pretty close to one another, and any conversation there could be heard by all. A man walked in, and the woman recognized him and said, "It's so good to see you again! How's everything?" He said, "Good…it's good to be back!" And she said "I almost didn't recognize you with that beard!" And then she said, "You looked so much better *WITHOUT* it!!" The silence in the room stopped when I cracked up laughing. They both turned and looked at me, and I just shrugged indicating that I couldn't help it! Hey, funny is funny!

...g in bed around 9:30 the other night...next to my hus-
...d watching some show on TV. I really don't remember exactly what
show...couldn't have been that exciting. Anyway, my husband often
falls asleep at this time, and the reason I know this is because he snores
a bit. Hey, when you're a Senior citizen, you have an absolute right to
snore! We live in Long Island, but I often wonder if his daughter - who
lives in California - ever hears his snores! *Kidding!* Anyway, there we
were, quietly watching the television when suddenly he flung his arm
out and smacked me right in the face! Thank goodness it really didn't
hurt, but I was absolutely shocked out of my mind! I'm sure you've
guessed by now that he was sound asleep...and this one time...he
WASN'T snoring! My scream woke him up, and he was so astounded
and sorry when I told him what happened. I couldn't stop laughing,
and I kept telling him that I was fine, but he had a lot of trouble falling
back asleep. Well...I guess that's what happens to you when you beat
your wife! Sorry dear...but funny is funny!

CPSIA information can be obtained
at www.ICGtesting.com
Printed in the USA
LVOW03s1140210817
545791LV00018B/941/P